More skills for a Brilliant Family Dog

D1440451

Fetch It!

Teach your Brilliant Family Dog to catch, fetch,
retrieve, find, and bring things back!

Beverley Courtney

Books by the author

New Puppy! From New Puppy to Brilliant Family Dog
How to survive the early weeks and still love your puppy!

Essential Skills for a Brilliant Family Dog

Book 1 Calm Down! Step-by-Step to a Calm, Relaxed, and Brilliant Family Dog

Book 2 Leave It! How to teach Amazing Impulse Control to your Brilliant Family Dog

Book 3 Let's Go! Enjoy Companionable Walks with your Brilliant Family Dog

Book 4 Here Boy! Step-by-Step to a Stunning Recall from your Brilliant Family Dog

Essential Skills for your *Growly* but Brilliant Family Dog

Book 1 Why is my Dog so Growly? Teach your fearful, aggressive, or reactive dog confidence through understanding

Book 2 Change for your Growly Dog! Action steps to build confidence in your fearful, aggressive, or reactive dog

Book 3 Calm walks with your Growly Dog. Strategies and techniques for your fearful, aggressive, or reactive dog

www.brilliantfamilydog.com/books

Your free book is waiting for you!

Get the next piece of the puzzle for your dog

Get the first digital book in the series,
Essential Skills for your Brilliant Family Dog
absolutely free here
https://www.brilliantfamilydog.com/freebook-calm-down

Disclaimer

I am not a vet!

I'm not a medic of any kind, so any opinions I express on anatomy or dangers are based on my best efforts to study the literature, from personal experience, and from case studies. Not gospel, in other words. In matters of your dog's health, defer to your vet.

Dogs learn just the same - whether big, small, male, female ... I switch from "he" to "she" on a whim.

All the photos in this book are of "real" dogs - either my own, or those of students and readers (with their permission). So the reproduction quality is sometimes not the best. I have chosen the images carefully to illustrate the concepts - so we'll have to put up with some fuzziness.

Contents

Introduction

When you first got your new dog you may have expected him to come with a retrieve installed. After all, don't all dogs love chasing balls and sticks?

Well no, actually, not all of them do!

You may have struck lucky and got a natural retriever, or you may have a dog that stares in puzzlement at anything you drop or throw - or simply runs off with it to demolish it. But all is not lost! You can teach your dog to love retrieving.

What is it?

But first let's look at what we mean by retrieve or fetch. Basically we want our dog to pick something up - whether dropped, found, or thrown - and bring it to us. Whether we want to chuck it again as a game (a frisbee, or a pine cone), open it and read it (the mail), wipe the slobber off and use it (car keys), we just want it brought to us. Preferably in one piece ...

Informal play retrieve

aka Fetch, Geddit, Where's your ball? and so on. This is all most of us will want. It's when we want to *play* with our dog - encouraging lots of running about and exercise, and as long as we come home with the same number of toys we left with, we don't really care if he runs about holding the toy, drops it in the mud, tosses it in the air, chomps it … It's his toy and his game.

This is a natural game for many dogs - but you'd be surprised how many have to be taught how to play it! Even dogs bred for generations to retrieve (think labradors, or spaniels) can become fearful or bewildered if we throw things and exhort them to bring them back.

Formal retrieve

Then there are formal retrieves, used by working dogs. These would include obedience competition dogs, gundogs, assistance dogs: we need the object brought to us without fuss and without being damaged. No toothmarks on the judge's retrieve article, no squashed birds, no chewed-up mail.

This is taught in a different way from the play retrieve - but the same dog can do both things! As you'll see as we get into this, she's perfectly able to distinguish between her ball and your phone, and act accordingly. We know how to put a plate on our lap and eat a sandwich with our fingers. We also know how to sit at a table and eat with cutlery - and manners! Your dog can make the same distinctions.

What will I learn in this book?

You'll be glad to know you're going to learn both types of retrieve! You may just want a play retrieve and be happy with that. But you'll have the option of also teaching your dog a formal retrieve, which opens the way to all the fun things she can do for you - like fetching the post, finding your tv remote, picking up things you've dropped when your hands are full - even if you never plan to compete or work your dog.

Two of my dogs act as quasi-assistance dogs. Not because I need help, but because we enjoy the extra interaction. So they can pick up their trailing lead, pull off my socks, fetch my jumper - and what I like best - anticipate when I need these things and suddenly appear with a shoe in their mouth, or a dinner bowl to be filled.

Instead of your dog being in the way and adding to your problems, he can be a real part of your life and help you solve those same problems. You can give him a job to do which he will be proud of.

This won't work for me - my dog is different ...

Yup. It will work for you.

Whether your dog is big or small, male or female, a herder or a guardian, a terrier or a toy, young or old, a pedigree or a crossbreed - it will work for you. You've already seen that I refer to your dog as "he" or "she" as the whim takes me. There's no difference in how they learn. One dog may be much faster than another, but as long as your dog is playing along enthusiastically, fetching and returning at a similar pace, he doesn't need to be a speed king.

Rome wasn't built in a day, and it may take time for a resistant retriever to learn the games. But he can and he will! Have patience ...

The only thing that can affect your dog's ability to retrieve is his physical make-up. If his mouth is so constructed that picking certain objects up is difficult (perhaps a very squashed-nose dog, or one with an undershot jaw or strange teeth) then you'll have to consider this in your choice of retrieve objects. But as long as a dog can eat - he can pick something up!

A word about Resource Guarding

One thing you'll learn is that you never snatch an article from your dog's mouth. That's not the way to treat a co-worker or family member! Apart from the fact that it isn't kind, you can actually create a Resource Guarding problem by pulling stuff away from your dog. He may say "That's mine!" and growl over his prize. This is nothing to do with discipline or reasoning - this is pure emotion and fear of loss. If this is a recurring problem, please get a force-free professional to help you, one-to-one. And meanwhile, never challenge a dog who is guarding something - just walk away. If you won't heed his growls, you may leave him no choice but to bite you.

Other helpful resources

While this book stands alone and you can teach your dog your retrieve here, you may find it helpful to check out the four books in the series Essential Skills for a Brilliant Family Dog. Here you'll find all the other parts of the puzzle, like locating your dog's off-switch, walking him nicely on the lead, getting an instant response when you call him, and teaching him not to hoover up everything he finds, whether tasty, disgusting, or dangerous!

Put together with this book and the New Puppy book if you're just beginning, and you have everything you need for dog-friendly training for your companion dog. When you visit the Resources section you'll find masses of things to help you with your dog.

Now dive in and get started!

1. Methods

So let's start off by looking at the two methods slightly more closely. We'll be going into detail with the learning later.

Play retrieve

This is the informal retrieve which is what most of us want with our dog. You can enjoy chucking a toy for her, enjoy watching her beauty as she races after it and snatches it out of the air, then it arrives back with you to throw again.

So this is a game you play for your and your dog's benefit. No-one is judging you or her. So if she wants to stamp on the toy, nudge it further to chase more, toss it in the air, chomp it, play tug with you before releasing it - that's all fine. You work out the game between you, and you reward what you find acceptable, and ignore what you don't.

Your retrieve game can also become a search game. It's really useful to teach this anyway, for when the toy really does appear to be lost, or - worse still - you're out in the middle of nowhere and your car keys have vanished! Twice recently my retrieving dogs have found someone's lost car keys for them in a huge field - to their astonishment and relief!

You don't have to have a retrieve to teach search - indeed for police dogs and other professional search dogs an "indication" is preferred, like a sit or a down, so as not to interfere with evidence. But unless you're a professional needing search capabilities in your dog, you can have your dog pick the article up if you like.

Chase!

The play retrieve is entirely based on the chase instinct which all dogs have to a greater or lesser degree. In some, prey drive and a strong chase instinct need to be tempered to ensure the safety of the local wildlife, cats and small dogs. In others it has to be teased awake to enable them to enjoy your games.

So a lot of what you'll be doing is reminding your dog that he's a fearless hunter, to focus on his prize - and to *geddit!* Once *you* get this it will become so much easier for your reluctant retriever to get it.

Formal retrieve

This is what you need for your working dog.

You could be working your dog in Competitive Obedience, Rally, or Working Trials. You could be training your gundog to work with you on a shoot. Or you could be training up your own Assistance Dog.

Your dog will need to learn how to pick up an item correctly without damaging it, he must hold it carefully in his mouth while he brings it to you, keep holding it till you ask for him to release it, then put it in your hand safely. He must wait till he's sent to fetch the article in the first place, then wait for further instruction once you've taken it.

This is very different from the play retrieve and needs a completely different way of teaching. But don't worry! The same dog can play boisterously with his toy then carefully bring you the tv remote. The one does not exclude the other.

So all those people who tell you you can't play fetch with your gundog are dwelling in the past when the only way of teaching was through force and coercion. There is no danger of your spaniel chewing up a bird just because he plays ball with you when off-duty!

Choice

And you'll achieve all this by the simple expedient of giving your dog a CHOICE. Instead of "Do this, do that," you'll be saying - just as you would to another respected family member - "Shall we do this, or would you prefer to do that?" For example, "If I drop your lead, would you like to bring it to me so we can continue our walk? It's up to you." "Would you like to go into your crate and chew your toy, or shall we play an exciting game with it, together?"

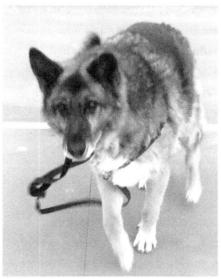

Viking brings his dropped lead

Of course - as all mothers know! - you weight the choices in your favour. Ideally you don't care which way your dog chooses, then you don't have an emotional investment in her "getting it right". All that tension will slip from your shoulders as you genuinely give your dog a choice, and watch with interest to see what she chooses.

One of the skills of this method is that when you offer a choice, you have to WAIT for the dog to make her decision. Give her time! We tend to bark commands and not wait to see what our pup thinks. Saying "Sit. Sit! Siddown. I said SIT …" is not giving her the courtesy of time to respond. We wouldn't speak to a visitor that way! We'd offer them a seat, then wait for them to choose one and park themselves. Your dog will soon find out that the "right" decision earns her something she likes, while the "wrong" decision gets her … nothing. (There's no blame or punishment involved in this - it's truly liberating all round!)

The joy of this method of training is that you never have to *tell* your dog to do anything! Later on, when he knows the words, you can *ask* him. But he learns entirely by doing. It's by doing that we all learn - would you learn to service a car by reading a book or listening to a lecture? No! You learn at your teacher's elbow, getting oil all over you and dropping tools in the wrong places. Just the same way you learnt to bake a cake with your mother, with mistakes and mess and laughter in your enjoyment of the process.

See what wise Confucius said, 2,000 years ago:

> I hear and I forget.
> I see and I remember.
> I do and I understand.

All Day Training

"Do I have to have set training sessions every day? I'm busy …" Of course you are - you're already using all the 24 hours in your day. So you may fear that if you don't fit training sessions in, things will start to slide and go wrong.

Never fear! If you're working with Choice Training, you'll be using **All**

Day Training. Every interaction with your dog is an opportunity for her to learn.

Do you line your children up each morning, and give them a potted 10-minute lecture on what they should or shouldn't do that day? Of course not! You teach them all the time, whenever you're interacting with them. Your young child asks for the plate of cake in your hand - you wait, staying still, till you get "Please!" then the child gets the cake. This is unconscious child-training, All Day Training, and you'll do the same with your dog.

- Every time he looks at you, you can reward him.
- Every time you take him to the garden, he can wait for you to open the door. Gradually he'll learn to sit when you touch the door handle, and when the door is wide open he'll wait to be released - you just start off with him finding that barging ahead doesn't open the door.
- Every time you feed him you have the opportunity to teach a little impulse control round something he desperately wants. Your dog waiting - even for a moment - is the same as your child saying Please.
- If you find him chewing the table-leg you can offer him something he's allowed to chew. He can choose to stay by the table not chewing, or go to his bed and enjoy his chew there.
- And so it goes on, all day. All Day Training. No big time-effort required.

Your new mantra!

To help you with this, I have a mantra for you to learn:

Reward what you like
Ignore what you don't like
Manage what you can't ignore.

So, EVERY time your dog does something you like, you mark it YES! and REWARD him.

Whenever he does something you don't like, you IGNORE it entirely. "I see no dog."

And in order to avoid situations which you can't ignore (e.g. dog is chewing your best shoes) you MANAGE things so that he can never get at your shoes (tidy them up!) - or anything else you value.

Once you adopt this method of working with your dog, you'll find that everything becomes so much easier! No senseless battles, no misunderstandings, no loss of patience for you, no frustration for the dog.

Learn the mantra, pin it up somewhere where the whole household can see it, and check frequently that you're following it, until it becomes second nature.

How to teach each retrieve

We'll be going in great detail, step-by-step, how to teach these. But first you need to learn the importance of how to let your dog know exactly when he's right - so on to the next chapter we go …

In this chapter we have learnt

- The difference between a play retrieve and a formal retrieve
- That chase is at the bottom of the retrieve
- It's all about Choice and rewards
- "I can play hard and work hard."

2. Rewards

Reward the choice you want your dog to make

So in order for Choice Training to work, you need to be able to mark the moment your dog does what you like - he makes the right choice, you reward that choice.

For example, if you're working on a speedy return with the item, you'll mark YES just as your dog turns towards you - this will encourage him to race to you for his reward. Result: fast return.

If you're working on getting him to pick up the toy, you'll start by marking YES when he just looks at it, and reward. Then you can up the ante and not mark till he nudges it with his nose, YES - reward. Get the idea? This is how he knows exactly what it was that you liked and that earnt him the reward. Now he knows to do it again.

Your timing is important - your YES must be instant! You can practice this by watching a clock hand ticking and saying YES as it moves, or when you toss a ball in the air, say YES the moment it pauses at its apex before falling again.

So what will you use as a reward?

This is not as simple as it may at first appear, and getting it right is critical!

What do *we* find rewarding?

If I did you a favour and you rewarded me with a big bowl of juicy oranges … I'd be unimpressed. I hate oranges. If, on the other hand, you had taken the time to notice that I love chocolate, and offered me a chocolate treat - I'd be asking you what else you'd like me to do!

So it's very important that you find out just what your dog loves and will sell his soul for! Effective rewards are anything your dog finds rewarding - play, cuddles, laughter, tasty treats, dinner, toys, running, chews, access to the garden - etc. Some of these are more suitable than others for training specific actions - laughter, tasty treats, toys, and running, spring to mind.

You don't need to establish superiority! Your dog knows which side her bread is buttered, and all she needs is kindness and patience while she works out what has a good outcome and what has no outcome worth pursuing.

Ensure that every action you like is marked and rewarded, and your dog will soon learn to repeat the things that earn her a reward and not bother with the things that don't.

Treats

Treats are without doubt the easiest way to reward your dog. But don't take this as the lazy option! There are efficient ways to get treats to work for you. And ways to ensure that they won't.

Personally, I avoid commercially-produced food almost entirely. When my children were growing I preferred to feed them with homemade food so I knew what was in it, and could make biscuits, for instance, the right size. The same goes for your dog. You can get great results by taking a couple of minutes to prepare some tasty treats - and it will normally work out much cheaper than shop-bought!

Cheese, sausages, hot dogs - chopped up very small (if you have a toy dog or puppy, then chopped up tiny) will work wonders with most dogs. You can have some in a container in the fridge so they're always ready. Make sure you always have good stuff to offer.

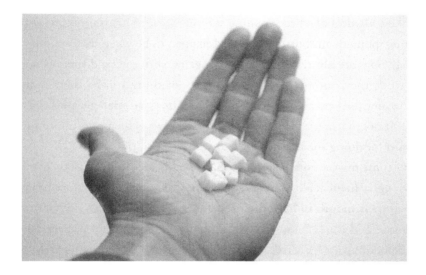

Notice your dog's response to the different treats you give her. Full attention, shiny eyes, cocked ears, swishing tail? You've hit the spot!

There are recipes all over the internet for homemade healthy dog treats. For training you need to make them small. For a puppy or small dog, *tiny*. You want this treat to go straight down so your dog's keen for the next one. No sniffing it suspiciously before taking it, no chewing for five minutes before swallowing it. He's now totally forgotten what you rewarded him for! YES is a distant memory!

Variety!

You can vary your rewards - perhaps kibble for the thing he's already good at, and top treats (cheese, sausage, etc) for the new thing. Always end with a game - even just "Chase me round the garden" is a good game - and make sure your session was very, very short. For a young puppy, ten treats or one minute is plenty; for a more experienced dog you could extend that to maybe three minutes. But not more. My own adult dogs are seldom worked for more than three minutes - and definitely not if it's something new they're learning. You want their response to stay enthusiastic and curious.

Having some good food ready chopped up in the fridge will make spontaneous sessions much easier. We all live very busy lives - there's no need to make a big deal of a little training session. Most of my training takes place in short, spontaneous bursts wherever I happen to be when the humour takes me. My dogs are always ready to have a game with me, and there is never a time when they cannot earn a reward for something I like - there is always food in my pocket, and also in small containers at strategic points in the house. It doesn't matter where we are, there's always the opportunity to earn a reward for doing something I like.

For some unaccountable reason, some people are stingy with their treats - or won't give them at all. Why? Did you know that killer whales can be taught to open their mouth to have their teeth cleaned, seagulls can carry a camera and locate and film enemy warships, giraffes in the zoo can present a leg to have blood drawn, chickens can run agility courses … and it's all taught using FOOD.

You want to become a treat-dispenser. I only give my dogs a treat when they've done something I like - so I aim to dish out a lot of treats in a day! They could fetch something for me, they could appear at my side on a walk, they could hurtle back when called from a rabbit-chase, they could pass a load of barking dogs behind a gate without reacting. The list is endless, and I want to capture every moment where my dog has made a good decision.

No NOOO!

And remember your mantra - that you are rewarding everything you like, and IGNORING everything you don't like! (I don't mean you ignore the dog - you ignore the thing that he's doing - big difference.) No NOOOO. No finger-wagging. No punishment of any kind. Punishment builds up resentment rather than the happy compliance we're looking for. And punishment doesn't just mean whacking your dog (heaven forbid). Think of speaking to someone and they simply turn away from you and cut you: this is punishing! They don't have to be rude or nasty, just dismiss you - and it's enough to upset you.

It's been proven scientifically over and over that if you reward something someone does, they're more likely to repeat that thing. Whereas if you punish them for what they do, they're less likely to repeat the action (when you're there and liable to punish them again). It doesn't hardwire the behaviour you want, just drives the bad behaviour underground for now.

If you were caught pinching a cake from the pantry as a child, I bet you made sure you weren't caught the next time! It didn't stop you stealing cakes, just made you devious.

Adding a vocal cue

We are vocal creatures and we think we have to take control and order people about. This extends to our children and our dogs. The wise parent (and the wise pet-owner) knows that this can lead to resistance and friction. Far easier to work along with the learner, then describe what they're doing as they do it. This is your vocal cue.

And note that you won't see me using the word "command" anywhere. Do you "command" your partner, or your work colleagues? I think not! Treat your dog with the same courtesy. *Ask* him to do something, don't *tell* him to. When you describe his action *as* he does it ("Sit," for instance), he'll associate that word with sitting (and a reward) and anticipate the action when you start to say it just before he sits.

So you have to get the action first, then you have all the time in the world to label that action with your chosen word or sound. Most people tend to do this backwards, and start with a word which is meaningless to our dog, expecting him somehow to know exactly what it means!

In fact, you're not going to find me explaining all this till you get right up to Chapter 8 - and NO! Don't jump there now! There's a reason these chapters are laid out in the order they are - it's to help you and your dog grasp this system in the easiest way.

Now you know how to reward your dog, let's look at what you're going to use to teach the retrieve.

In this chapter we've learnt:

- Not everyone likes the same things
- You need to find what your dog loves
- Your timing with YES is critical
- "How can I make my owner say YES again?"

3. Retrieve articles

While you may only want your dog to retrieve his frisbee, or a dumbell in competition, it's a good idea to get him used to lots of different shapes and textures from early on. Starting with your young puppy is ideal, and mine find all kinds of things scattered on the floor for them to interact with. Plastic things, squashy things, soft toys, crunchy toys, metal teaspoons, cardboard cartons, and so on. We want them to explore these things with their mouths and find that touching them or picking them up is rewarding: YES! = reward.

You can do this with an older dog too. Your dog may have learnt to leave things alone for fear of getting into trouble, so you want to make it clear that these are things you *want* him to interact with!

Play retrieve articles

For your play retrieve, you can use absolutely anything! (Well, almost anything - see the section on dangerous items below.)

- Never admonish your dog for picking up something you don't want him to have - if you tell him off once for picking something up you're going to have to spend a lot longer teaching him that he can! Simply swap the item for a treat and thank him.
- *Never* chase your dog to get something from him: this is a terrific game called *Keepaway* and will give your dog hours of fun! Ask him to come for a super treat or toy - hold the treat to his nostrils and take the item when he drops it so he can eat the treat.

So in addition to the items listed above for the puppy, you can have knotted socks, the inner tube from a kitchen roll, balls, frisbee, their dinner bowl. I favour soft hollow balls, like a tennis ball, for safety and comfort. And for frisbees I prefer the soft-rimmed ones which are easy on the mouth. You don't want your dog coming back dripping blood from his mouth from the sharp edges of a chomped plastic frisbee. Some of the stiff ones cement themselves flat to the ground too, so your dog is unable to get a purchase on them. So comfort and ease of pick-up are the order of the day. Balls on ropes are winners here, as you can easily catch the rope to release from the mouth, rather than having to handle a slimy, drooly ball!

From the outset you'll be teaching your dog to hold the item without inflicting mortal wounds on it - or your fingers as you reach for it. I won't take the offered toy unless the dog's mouth is still - I just take my hand away. Any chomping delays the release and the continuation of the game.

Formal retrieve articles

Most Obedience-type competitions have the dog retrieving a dumbell in the lower classes. This has the advantage of being easy to pick up and that it slips easily into the correct position in the mouth. So the opportunities for scrabbling for the article and chomping and squeezing with the teeth are minimised from the start. The dumbell size and fit is important. It wants to sit comfortably in the mouth, with the bar in the gap behind the canines, and the side pieces not pressing against the dog's lips or cheeks. It needs to be a snug fit though, so it can't slide from one side to the other as your dog moves his head.

From here they'll graduate to more awkward articles - something long that needs to be balanced in the mouth, something dangly to trip over, something toy-like to provoke the unwanted chewing, and also the scent cloths used in scent discrimination.

This is why it's essential from the outset to teach your pro dog to hold the article gently and correctly - more in the step-by-step chapter. So consideration of the articles is important. I favour a short hard tube to start with. Until he's very experienced you want to choose articles that will help him hold them correctly - not use the tricky ones some judges like to offer in the higher classes. And don't experiment with your extremely expensive electronic car keys till you know you have a soft hold!

As in all learning interactions with your dog, remember to be *teaching*, not *testing*. Testing suggests you will keep going till the exercise breaks down, while teaching means you are always helping your dog to succeed.

Food toys

In your search for the perfect retrieve, don't overlook the power of FOOD in the teaching! Some people have a strange resistance to using food in training, though I've no idea why. They seem to be stuck in some Victorian schoolroom where children and dogs had to do what they were told, just because. Modern education methods and the science of Learning Theory have proved over and over again, without question, that rewarding the behaviour you like is the way to get the quickest and most enthusiastic results.

Remember those giraffes, seagulls and killer whales from Chapter 2?

> *You have to feed your dog anyway, so why not get some mileage from that food and speed up your training?*

Toys that you can conceal food in will be very helpful for the reluctant retriever. These could be commercial toys (a Lotus ball, preferably on a rope, is a good example) where your dog rips open the velcro (very gratifying sensation for the dog!) and can reward himself. You may have to start off by opening the toy yourself to show him how. Budget version: an old sock, knotted, containing something scrummy and smelly and enticing. If it's raw liver or sardines, you can chuck it away after one use and find another. Hint - under a teenager's bed is the best place to look for old socks.

Here's a nice story about Charlie the reluctant retriever:

> "I would like some advice on how to teach Charlie to fetch as he does not seem at all interested in returning thrown items nor holding on to them for even a short period of time. It doesn't seem instinctive to him." Kevin and Charlie, Spaniel

After I gave Kevin some advice about how to use food toys, this is what he wrote:

> "With your advice, and the toy you suggested, we have success. Charlie is eager to return to hand any thrown items on demand. Thanks again."

Dangers of everyday articles!

While found articles like sticks and pine cones seem a good way to start - especially with a play retrieve - there are some things you need to consider before choosing these.

Sticks should only ever be thrown *either* into water, *or* where you can be absolutely sure they will land on the ground long before the dog reaches them. Horrendous impalement injuries have been caused by a dog racing towards a stick that lands as he arrives. Other than that a stick is ok unless your dog sees it as a chew toy. This is not going to help your retrieve, and may damage his insides.

Pine cones are fine as long as you haven't got a chewer. My Border Collie Rollo will find a pine cone or stick if no other toy is offered, but he never chews them so it's not a problem. Pine cones dropped at my feet can be kicked for him, sticks are always ignored unless we're at a pond and he's swimming for them.

Rollo launches into the pond for a stick

It's good to see him balance a long stick or branch so he holds it right in the middle, and fun to watch him negotiate his way through a kissing gate with one! He's learnt to drop it before going through, then to push the swing gate back over it so he can pick it up again from the other side. He gets much enjoyment from handling awkward articles and solving such problems, and this may never have happened if he hadn't been encouraged to play with a variety of objects as a puppy, then taught how to handle them as he got older.

Other hazardous toys could include:

- The balls you launch with a plastic "arm". I've often been surprised by a dog hurtling towards my group chasing a ball that the owner has thoughtlessly chucked right at us: fast evasive action needs to be taken before the dog comes stampeding in! As operating this launcher requires so little effort, and the ball can be thrown so far, people often don't realise how exhausted their dog may be getting. Some dogs will literally keep going till they drop. In a recent unaccustomed heatwave here in England it was awful to see hapless dogs being run ragged and risking collapse from heatstroke, by owners absentmindedly chucking their ball further and further, while they texted on their phones, or gazed into space. This is not a companionable walk!

- Hard balls, or any ball of a size that could lodge in your dog's throat: better to have it too big than too small. I would only use balls with holes in, or squashy hollow balls that you could stab to remove in an emergency. Balls on a rope score here.
- Any object that could land with a spike or protrusion uppermost for the dog to run onto.
- Anything which can degrade when bitten hard and leave sharp metal or plastic shards sticking out.
- There is evidence that a dog skidding to pick up a ball from the ground can damage his shoulders. For this reason I prefer them to catch balls on the bounce, or frisbees from the air above them, or be able to chase a rolling frisbee and snatch it up on the run. It takes a little skill to throw your dog's toy in such a way that he won't injure himself getting it. You'll have to practice as well as your dog!

My dog wears a muzzle

That's ok - he can still enjoy his retrieve games! You'll need to find a toy with a string or small handle that he can poke through the bars of his muzzle and hold with his front teeth.

Oscar so loves his toy that he can pick it up through his muzzle

In this chapter you have learnt

- Which articles to use for each type of retrieve
- How to accustom your dog to variety early on
- Safe vs unsafe toys
- "I can still play fetch with my muzzle on!"

4. Teach your dog to catch

Jake is still athletic enough at 14 years old
to pluck his frisbee out of the air

My dogs are great catchers. I get huge pleasure from watching their athleticism and joy. But they didn't come with catching installed: this skill was carefully nurtured and developed!

Teaching your dog to catch is an essential for the play retrieve. It opens the door to frisbee-catching, and even catching soft balls. Many dogs absolutely love catching, so it's fun to teach anyway.

Start with close catches

If you're starting with a puppy, wait till he's 16 weeks or so - and preferably once he knows lots of games featuring treat-rewards as well as chasing down toys. A very young pup (up to around 10 weeks) doesn't spot or focus on things very quickly. We're going to start with catching food - no jumping or leaping about required as you're going to aim it very carefully at his mouth!

To teach your dog eye-mouth co-ordination, make it easy for him by always tossing your treat with the same arm movement. I favour the downward toss - i.e. you hold up your hand near your shoulder, wave it a bit to get your dog's attention, then slowly bring it downwards and release the treat so it loops down to the dog. Aim for the top of his muzzle, right where the nose leather begins. The more accurate your throws the faster he'll get it.

This is the entertaining bit! To begin with the treats will bounce off his muzzle and he'll scramble to get them off the floor.

Eventually his mouth will start to open as the treat comes through the air. And after a lot of practice at this, he'll actually catch one! He'll probably be more surprised than you and start hunting on the floor for it again, not realising it's in his mouth!

You can make it a lot easier for him by using treats that are clear to see - so little cubes of pale cheese are good. With one particularly slow-to-catch-on adult dog I used popcorn (plain, of course). And while corn should not generally form part of a dog's diet, an exception can occasionally be made to get what you want. The popcorn worked for that dog because it's huge, white, and floats down slowly.

At this stage you could be feeding your dog's whole dinner this way, one tossed piece of kibble at a time.

Once your dog can catch a flying treat aimed carefully at his nose, you can start tossing them at different angles. An adult dog (especially a greedy one!) will become quite athletic getting his treats. Take care that he's on a firm footing, not a slippery floor. And build up slowly towards jumping.

Now add your frisbee

Now you've got the treat-catch mastered, you can move up a gear and start teaching your dog to catch a frisbee. Of course you can use any toy you like, as long as it is soft and easy to catch.

If you go for a frisbee, you need a soft one that is gentle on the mouth and teeth - one made for dogs. A light fabric one with a soft tube inside the rim is ideal. I like these so much that when they're unavailable here in the UK I order several from the States to keep us going for a while. It's soft on the mouth, easy to squash into a pocket, and floats beautifully in the air for controlled catching.

Now using the same idea as with the cheese, you float the frisbee towards your dog *who is right in front of you.* So we're talking about a couple of feet from hand to nose. No distance yet. After a lot of failed attempts he'll be catching the frisbee expertly by the rim. If the frisbee is not inherently rewarding for him, you can treat him when he catches it - this will cause him to let go of it.

If he's not inclined to release the frisbee, or wants to run off with it, simply stand on his lead so he can't, then swap it for a treat every time. Once he's got that, you can change your reward from treat to instant throw. He'll soon know that the routine of "catch then give" means you'll throw it again immediately. So he'll be anxious to hand it over straight away.

Now start adding a little distance - maybe a yard to start with.

And gradually grade up over a number of lessons. As you increase the distance, you'll build your own skill with the frisbee. A flick of the wrist is what's needed to spin it, rather than brute force. And one of the reasons I like those soft cloth frisbees is because they're so easy to spin and send over large distances.

Now you have a way to exercise your dog safely while enjoying the sight of him flying after his frisbee and catching it expertly, bringing it straight back to you and pushing it into your hand - to throw again!

Safety note

There are dogs who do amazing antics catching their frisbee in competitions. But I have to say these images and videos make me very uneasy. The gyrations and hard landings look to me as if they'd take their toll pretty quickly on these dogs. I like to take life easier - and have my dogs last longer - so I aim to float the frisbee over the dog's head, so that he can leap through an arc to catch it, landing comfortably and carrying on running.

I look for fast running, an athletic leap, a soft landing - and I ensure that we're not working on parched or frozen ground that would be too hard to land on.

Remember this is another golden opportunity to teach some impulse control. Your dog will never get the frisbee by snatching it from your hand, or leaping up to mug you for it. He has to wait while you prepare to throw. You may want him to sit and wait, lie down and wait, or you may be happy for him to hurtle out twenty yards in the direction you're about to throw it - your choice. Similarly, when you put out your hand for the frisbee to be delivered, it should be pushed into your hand - and not snatched away again!

Multiple dogs?

Each of my dogs has his or her own frisbee. This means that

- I too get a great workout as my arms are going like a windmill, collecting and throwing frisbees one after the other, and
- There's never a collision or scrap over possession of the toy. They only go for their own toys.

While my two older dogs will carry their frisbee for the entire walk without losing it, the two younger ones can get distracted and drop it somewhere. So teaching a search is also useful so that they find it instead of me spending ages looking for it. You'll learn about this in Chapter 9. Rollo my Border Collie is brilliant at finding toys, and will lie down next to one (while his own is firmly clamped in his mouth) until it's restored to its owner.

Another supreme virtue of the dogs loving their frisbee: I can re-focus them very easily from incoming dogs to avoid confrontations. So if you have a reactive or growly dog, get him mad about retrieving as soon as possible!

In this chapter we've learnt:

- How to teach a reliable catch
- The type of toy to use
- How to work with several dogs at once
- "This is a wonderful game!"

5. Step-by-step Play retrieve

Coco Poodle is happily holding a teaspoon - at only 8 weeks old!

So now, here we go! Let's get started on teaching your dog how to play fetch with you.

For most of you, this will be enough - you don't need a formal competition-type retrieve. But don't worry, if you want to compete with your dog later on, or train her up as your assistance dog - you won't have broken anything! You can still teach her later to fetch your phone or your car keys without smashing them to smithereens.

Though I don't mind my dogs tossing their toy in the air, digging at it, or turning it round in their mouth as they return when we're *playing,* I still teach them to pick up cleanly and hold it firmly from the start.

Ready, get set, play!

The essence of this method is that it's fun! It's a game! So get your dog playing with you first. If she'll tug, do that. If she'll run after toys, do that - whether she brings them back or not. And if toys are not *de rigueur* yet, just run about and play chase and dodge with her. You want to get her heart rate up a bit so she doesn't fall asleep when you want to work with her.

1. Where you start this is important. Skip the busy kitchen or distracting garden. The best place to start is the study, spare bedroom, or bathroom or any other small room which is free of distraction.

2. Kneel on the floor if you are able. This stops you looming over your dog, which many find very intimidating. Or you can sit so the dog is just in front of you.

3. Animate your chosen toy - *at ground level*. You want to simulate a rat or rabbit moving fast, then stopping to twitch its whiskers, then darting forward again. A kind of figure of eight movement on the floor around you will work. Watch your dog - he'll suddenly plug into this movement as his instincts wake up. Then he'll start to chase it.

4. He may start by pouncing on it, and using his feet to stop it. Keep it moving, jerking it away as he gets close, until he realises he can use his mouth for this. Let him catch it! And mark with a YES.

Coco catches the moving toy

5. And immediately reward him with a treat to his nostrils, removing the toy as he releases it (you were still holding on to it!)

6. Repeat, repeat, repeat, till you are actually both holding the article for a moment before you ask for a release. This is your first session and will probably take you about three minutes. STOP! Don't be tempted to carry on till your dog gets bored and loses interest! Remember we're teaching, not testing. Put the toy away and have another go later.

7. Next session, run through what you did the first time. Then keep going, for another max three minutes. By now your dog should be keen to see the toy, should get excited and want to pounce and grab straight away. Good! Get to the stage when she's holding it for a little bit longer before your YES and reward. You can use "Thank you" instead of "Yes" if you wish, your word means "Drop the toy, I have a treat for you." Keep this all moving very fast, don't dawdle between the play. When she's holding the toy, stop moving it. We're not playing Tug here - more about that later. We want her just to enjoy the sensation of possession of the object in her mouth before you thank her and reward her. It doesn't matter at all if she drops it. You will get better at catching it when she releases!

8. Once she'll catch the snaking toy on the ground - holding it for a moment (and I mean *just a moment* … maybe two seconds) then release it on your vocal cue (Thank you or Yes) - you can move on. Be honest about this! Don't race ahead till you've got this going right - it won't help you and will just cause confusion for your poor dog. Got that? Ok, now put your hand round her chest, snake the toy about then toss it a foot or so away. She should pull against your hold to get the toy - immediately release and let her grab it from the ground, YES - treat. End after a couple of these grabs. She should still be bright-eyed and bushy-tailed! If she's bored, you went on way too long. Shorter next time!

9. It's a simple task now to translate the article grab from the floor to in the air, and to extend the time she's holding it. First the hold: you want to be sure

to ask for the toy to be released *before* she even considers chomping it. This means you may take quite a while to extend this duration. That's ok. It'll happen gradually. You don't want her to squeeze or crunch it because you asked her to hold it too long. Work fast, be ready to mark (Thank you or Yes) and feed quickly so she never gets this idea of tightening her hold. Keep your session short.

I say YES and catch Cricket's toy as she drops it

10. You can toss the toy along the floor a little further sometimes, so that when you release your chest-hold she plunges forward to pick it up. This enthusiasm to launch after the toy is an important attitude to bake in to your play retrieve from the start. Only gradually build distance of the throw, sometimes close up, sometimes further away. As long as the burst forward and the enthusiasm to grab it and race back to you with it is retained, you've got it!

11. Now you can hold it just off the floor for her to hold, and gradually have it up at her head level and offer it to her to hold. This part is not so important for the play retrieve, though it's useful. The recipe for tossing it for her to catch in the air can be seen in Chapter 4.

12. Did you rush? Keep in mind that this is a slow build. It takes as long as it takes. For some dogs that will be very quick - just a few sessions. For others, who say, "Why are you doing this to me?" it may take quite a while. Don't worry, we're all different. Go at a pace at which you can see gradual improvement.

Perfection

So you now have a dog who is keen to go into the small training area with you and your toy. She's alert and ready to engage. She grabs the toy as soon as she's released, holds it without chomping for a short while, then releases on your vocal cue. She can catch when it's tossed to her right in front of you, and is happy to continue the game.

Yes?

No?

Ok, let's look at some things you may be coming up against …

Troubleshooting

Q My dog has ZERO interest in the toy. She just sits and stares at me.

A It's up to you to make this game exciting! Maybe she's been told not to touch things in the past, or not to chase. You are reversing that and giving her permission to do both those things. Extend your playtime before you start till you're both puffing and gasping for breath, then do a quick wiggle with the toy on the ground, snatch it away and finish. Keep doing this till she alerts to the toy and takes an interest. It *will* come, really! Also refer back to the section on foodtoys in Chapter 3. Many reluctant retrievers have become avid chasers once they discover the joy of the foodtoy!

Q We started well, but when he found I had treats in my hand he wanted those, and spat the toy out!

A Speed will work for you here. And keeping the treats in a pot behind you, not in your hand. Say your release cue (Thank you or Yes) as soon as he has the article in his mouth, let him drop it on the floor or into your hand, then you pass him a treat. You can slowly make the time before you speak slightly longer. We are working with Choice Training, so he needs to learn that if he wants the treat he has to hang on to the article. Not asking too much to begin with will help him "get" this.

Q Ha! He grabs the toy alright - then legs it, with me chasing behind.

A Are you working in a small space as suggested? If this isn't possible, than put a long lead on him and stand on it, so he can't get away - then "Thank you!" and treat to nose. If you don't want something to happen, don't let it happen! Much easier to prevent than cure. If this dog is more interested in toys than treats, try working with two toys. As soon as he gets one you relax your pull (bunny dead) and waggle the other about on the floor. He'll spit out the first to get the second, live, one.

Q She grabs the toy - then that's the end of the game!

A Ok, you want to work with mega-exciting treats that only appear when you go into this little room with your dog and the toy. Steak? Liver? Roast chicken? Smoked cheese? Cold pasta? Something irresistible. Then hold the tasty morsel to your dog's nostrils and give it to her. Do this a few times before introducing the toy, then do the same. She will drop the article and take the treat … sooner or later. Have patience.

Q My dog is LOVING this! Trouble is, he grabs the toy, releases it nicely, then snatches it back. He's caught my fingers a couple of times.

A Ouch! Have a couple of pieces of food in your hand when you reward him. First one for letting go, then the second one to keep him engaged while you put the toy behind your back. Then immediately present the toy again, at whatever stage you're at - wiggling, tossing, throwing. It should only take a few reps before he realises this actually makes the game go faster! The sooner he releases the toy the sooner he can play again.

Q She grabs the toy, spins round and throws it at my feet.

A I like this enthusiasm. Be quick and have your hand ready to catch it as soon as she picks it up. Speed is important with the quick dog. You want to get in there first with what *you* want to happen before she does what *she* thinks is meant to happen! As soon as she realises she doesn't have to throw it at you to get rewarded, you can start extending the duration of the hold. Do keep chatting to your dog - "Oh you clever dog, you're holding it now!" This will focus her on you for a moment while she still holds it.

Q I'm commanding her to release it, but she doesn't.

A Take another look at *Adding a vocal cue* in Chapter 2, Rewards. We only use a word once the dog is doing what we want. "Thank you" or YES means "I like what you did, you have earnt a reward." Practice this frequently with no retrieve article involved. Just Thank you - treat, Thank you - treat. She'll soon get the message and let go of the article to get her reward. Forget about "commands"! This is a game between the two of you.

Q I've been doing this for several days now. Some days he's got it and some days - no clue.

A This will take time! Rome wasn't built in a day. And if you're working with an older dog who has never picked things up, it'll take longer than with a puppy you've been encouraging to hold toys from the get-go. Keep a Retrieve Diary and just make a note of where you're at and how keen he is. This will stop you racing ahead and expecting too much. Learning is not a linear graph! We understand more, then less, depending on lots of outside factors, like weather, digestion, mood, tiredness. Make allowances for this. Another good way to keep a record is to prop up your smartphone and video your session. You'll probably see loads of things that you've introduced that aren't in the list above. *Stick to the program!*

Q We were doing really well, then he just lay down and gave up.

A Did you go on a bit too long? Just three reps may be enough in the early stages. Don't bore your dog! Maybe he's just tired today. Maybe *you're* tired or anxious about something and he's picking up on this and thinking he's doing something wrong. Lighten up, take a break, and start from scratch when you're both in the mood and playing excitedly already.

In this chapter we have learnt:

- A step-by-step process to teaching your dog a play retrieve
- It's easier than you may have thought
- Don't get stuck - there's always a way
- "This game is fun!"

6. Tug

14-week-old Zoe chases the "rabbit"

I love all my dogs to learn to tug. It's the Best Game Ever for them, and they absolutely love it. And no, they never grab my sleeve or my hand. They just use their own tug toys.

Won't this ruin my retrieve?

But I can hear some of you protesting already! And I'll address your protests straight away.

The objection to playing this game arises from a misunderstanding. It assumes the dog cannot distinguish between the toy and you. Or your sleeve. Or your child. It assumes that the dog who can pick up a young puppy so gently will become incapable of controlling herself and start ragging everything she finds.

If you give me a biscuit, I know to bite it. If you give me an ice cream, I know to lick it. Your dog has the exact same powers of distinguishing between objects!

You can see in these pictures that Lacy can clearly distinguish between the two actions *on the same toy*. When I ask her to tug, she tugs like a demon and stops instantly on cue. When I ask her to hold, she holds it gently in her mouth without biting down on it.

Want to view the whole video? You'll find it at
www.brilliantfamilydog.com/retrieve

Once you've taught the Hold (for gentle hold) or Geddit (for tug) you'll also teach the Give and you'll add vocal cues to these actions. The fact that my dogs will fetch my shoes or jumper for me when I ask does not mean that they keep finding shoes and clothes and presenting me with them when they're not asked!

These images alone should convince you that depriving your dog (and you) of the pleasure of playing tug is unnecessary. Old-fashioned gundog trainers forbid toy-games with their dogs. What a shame! Why deny your dog his self-expression through his instinctive drives?

What Tug to use?

First off, what do you use for playing tug? Well you can use absolutely any soft fabric, rope, or leather item that is long enough to keep teeth one end and your hand the other. A soft tug won't hurt your dog's mouth - particularly important in a young puppy - and it's easy to stuff in a pocket.

I have a number of different tuggies - homemade, plaited fleece, real fur or sheepskin, long ones, shorter ones - all sorts.

Different dogs prefer different types, so test them out on your dog to find his preference. The very long ones allow group-tug with several dogs at once!

You'll find that Tug is a great way to teach impulse control. Your dog will be excited and highly aroused - and that is when he'll find it hardest to listen to you and follow your requests. Keeping it within a structure makes it easier for him to understand and comply. Then this can translate to other times of high arousal.

And why Rules? Well, all games have rules. If you were playing tennis with me and I insisted on standing the same side of the net as you, or hitting all the balls out of the court, that wouldn't be much of a game. Even small children know this, and you'll hear them making up a game and inventing the rules as they go along - "You have to stand on one leg," and "You're not allowed to touch the table," for example. Getting the rules straight ensures understanding - and freedom to enjoy the game fully.

Here's how you teach your dog Tug, with safety built in!

9 Rules for playing Tug

1. It's *your* toy. You allow your dog to play with it when you want, and only if he keeps to the rules. Because it's never left on the floor, and the only time your dog gets to play with the tug is with you on the end, it becomes a very high-value toy.

2. You are harnessing a very strong instinctive drive in your dog - to stalk, chase, pounce, capture, shake and kill his prey - and turning it to your advantage instead of trying to work against it.

3. When playing, always keep the tuggie low on the floor - this is to prevent your pup jumping and injuring himself, it also keeps the teeth pointing downwards and he's less likely to grab your hand or sleeve.

4. Start by snaking the tuggie around on the floor, like a rabbit - stop, twitch whiskers, run - this is what stimulates the chase instinct and is the signal to play. You never let go of the tug.

5. Encourage him to grip tight on the tug - have a great game, but don't be too rough or hurt his mouth. Exert the same amount of pull as your dog does - it's an equal game. And pull directly away from him, low down, keeping all his feet on the floor. Don't rattle him about on the end of the tug or lift him up with it! Growling is part of the game.

6. If his teeth touch your hand or sleeve, your dog will be aware, so yelp to interrupt him, put tug behind your back, and wait for calm before offering it again. He should now be much more careful. If he's over the top, put the toy away till later.

7. When you're ready, relax your pull so the tuggie goes limp (rabbit now dead) and hold a treat to your dog's nose. As he lets go to eat the treat, put the tuggie behind your back (don't take it past your face!). The reward for letting go? Your dog gets to play again!

8. Bring the tug out from behind your back, hold it out in front of you and tease him a little with it. If he tries to jump or grab it, it goes straight behind your back (never past your face). Repeat till he shows that he wants it but is not jumping or grabbing (he doesn't have to sit, but he can if he wants), then *immediately* whack it to the floor - game on!

9. As you both become more expert at this game - which should become your dog's top favourite - you can use the cue "Geddit" as you whack the tuggie to the ground, and "Give" as your empty hand approaches his nose.

TROUBLESHOOTING

Q My dog keeps letting go then grabbing again and catching my fingers

A He would go hungry pretty quickly in the wild if he didn't learn to hang on to his prey once he'd caught it! So if he lets go, you whip the toy away behind your back then re-offer it. He only gets to tug if he's maintaining pressure and holding on to it firmly.

Q I always understood that I have to win the game - that the dog mustn't get the tug?

A If you're playing together, you need to be holding on to your end of the tuggie. But there's no need for you always to take it off him. If he's really excited at getting his "prey" you can let him enjoy it for a bit - strutting around trophying it, or rattling it and "breaking its neck" - then ask for it and start the game again. The only time this wouldn't work well is if your dog starts to resource guard the article - showing the whites of his eyes and going still or snarling. This means that you need to do some work on his impulse control around things he wants *in general.* Resource guarding isn't common, but you may need professional help to kindly change this.

Q My dog loves this game, but he growls a lot. Is this ok?

A I encourage growling and excitement in Tug. You can growl back! As long as your dog lets go when you release pressure and ask him for the toy, it's all part of the game.

Q When I go to pull it out of his mouth he won't let go

A When you want your dog to release, release your pressure on the tug as you hold a treat to his nostrils. Just stay still, *no pulling,* and you'll see your dog begin to change his grip on the tug (the rabbit is dead). As he does this you can ease the tug out of his mouth a little each time he adjusts his hold. Don't pull or he'll think the rabbit has come back to life and needs to be restrained! If your dog is still not letting go, even with a treat on the nose and no pulling, you can use the collar method. Slip your hand in his collar and keep your arm straight. You are *not* pulling his collar, just ensuring that he can't pull back any more on the tug. Then wait and ease it out of his mouth, as above, each time he relaxes his jaws. Be patient!

Q My puppy is about 5 months old and teething - there was blood on the tug!

A Tug is a great way to shift teeth that are not dropping out on their own. They'll soon ping out with a bit of light tugging! If your pup's mouth is sore, let him decide if he wants to tug or not, then leave the game for a week or two till he's keen to play. Don't pull it too vigorously or twist him around on the tug.

Q I have a gundog, I've been told I can't play Tug

A Sigh. There's that misbelief again. There's a world of difference between picking up a dead bird and holding it in the (specially-adapted) gundog mouth, and pulling vigorously on something that is trying to escape. Play is how we learn, and Tug is a wonderful way for your dog to learn control of his mouth - Bite Inhibition. A world-class sheepdog trainer told me that all his best dogs were great at playing football with the kids. Poking the ball with his mouth, or pushing it with his chest, did not make the dog start bullying the sheep! Rather it gave him an outlet for his natural behaviour.

Q I've been using his ball on a rope, which he loves chasing. But he won't hold on

A Those balls are often very hard or knobbly, and not easy to hold on to when pulled or slimy. You can use the same toy, just hold the ball yourself and let him pull on the rope handle!

In this Chapter we've learnt:

- Tug is the best game ever!
- Tug will not spoil your retrieve
- It's the quickest way to teach impulse control
- "Oh yeah! I love tugging!"

7. Step-by-step FORMAL retrieve

A smart return with the retrieve article

I trust that by now you've got at least partway to enjoying vigorous games of catch, tug, and fetch with your dog! If not yet, just keep building and it will grow.

Applications for the formal retrieve

I want to take a look at teaching the formal retrieve - for competition dogs and assistance dogs - pointing up the differences between it and the play retrieve, and showing you how the same dog can most definitely do both as required.

Most dog competitions started out life heavily influenced by the professional dog-handlers of the day, mostly police dog handlers. In this work, preserving the evidence is key, so working police dogs are largely taught to indicate a find by sitting or lying down, rather than contaminate the evidence by picking it up. Where they do use their mouths, of course, is for bitework - stopping a criminal on the run. They are taught to grip cleanly and firmly and not let go till told to release. This is, in fact, a kind of retrieve - with a large wriggling retrieve article!

In dog competitions (Obedience, Rally, Working Trials, for instance) the dog has to be under step-by-step control in the retrieve section. No independent thought required here! Just step-by-step, getting each stage accurate, for maximum marks. Mouthing the article, tossing it, dropping it, fiddling with it, a messy pick-up - are all heavily downmarked. Gundogs also may not mess with the competition dummy and have to work with it as gently as with the bird it simulates.

Assistance dogs also need to learn this skill, as often they will be asked to pick things up which are delicate or breakable - and who wants their shoes to arrive filled with dribble?

So you can see that the first consideration of the formal retrieve is that the item should be picked up cleanly, carried carefully, and delivered to hand on cue. This isn't a game - though dogs still enormously enjoy this work and get great pleasure from doing it just right!

And to achieve this, we're going to start at the end and work backwards. This is known in the trade as back-chaining, and is a practice not confined to dog training.

Many years ago our school choirmaster would introduce us to a new piece by starting on one of the most difficult yet exciting passages. Only after we were familiar with this would he then take us through from the start. When we reached the tricky passage, instead of falling apart and saying "Oh this is too hard!", we thought "Hey, we know this!" and launched into it easily. And this is the effect we'll get with your dog too.

Let's get started!

1. Like the play retrieve, you want to work in an area without distractions. These concepts may be hard for your dog to grasp, so you need his full

attention. So a small quiet room is ideal. You'll need a ready supply of top-quality, quick-to-swallow treats, your chosen articles (see Chapter 3), and - if your dog loves play retrieve, one of his play articles to finish up with. If your dog is large enough to sit in front of you with his head above your knee level, then you can sit. You'll want to sit forward in your chair so he can get right in between your knees. If he's tiny, try putting him on a table or tall dog bed so you can work together easily.

2. You want to start at the end of your sequence, which is releasing the article. But hang on! How can he release it before he's got it in his mouth? Good question! We do the two together.

You can teach this with his carefully-fitted dumbell. But if your dog is daunted by this strange-looking beast, just use a hard tube, without the side parts of a dumbell. The tube needs to be hard so that the dog does not find pleasure in squeezing or crunching it, as he may with a card tube or wooden dowel. This mouthing does not have to be *stopped* - it must never be allowed to happen! This may mean that you have to work very fast with your give and take so your dog doesn't get the opportunity to explore the article with his teeth.

I favour a hard tube to start off with, easy to slip a finger in to hold it. It needs to be long enough to protrude from the side of the dog's mouth so you can hold on to it.

Lacy holds the tube just behind her canines

a. With your dog sitting in front of you (ready warmed up as for the play retrieve, knowing you have good treats, ready to learn) and slightly between your knees for your comfort, pick up your tube, holding it in front of you, and show it to him. He looked at it, of course! YES - treat, removing the tube from view. Then produce it again - he looks, YES - treat, remove from view.

By the way, if you like to use a clicker instead of YES, by all means do so. It's all in the timing. Your YES and your click both mean "I like what you did, you have earned a reward." Either way it's essential to mark the split second your dog does the thing you want so he knows what to repeat.

b. Now that your dog knows that this little tube signifies good things, you want to move from just a look to a nose touch. In fact you're going to move through a sequence of look/sniff/nose-touch/nose-press/teeth-touch/open mouth/lick/hold. So after a few deliberate looks and YES/treats, you hold out your article to your dog, your dog looks at it, and you WAIT. As it's right there, in front of him, he's most likely to sniff it - or at least lean towards it. YES - treat. Repeat a few times. Work fast. Keep your dog's focus.

c. This is where you're going to graduate to a nose-touch. Sooner or later - usually sooner - while you're waiting, your dog will say "I AM looking at it, can't you see?" and bop it with his nose to prove it. Success! YES - treat. Repeat this stage a few times.

d. Next we want the teeth to touch the article. Nose-bopping is good and has been rewarded up to now. Now we move the goalposts again, ever so slightly! Hold out the article, get a nose-bop, WAIT. Your dog is likely to look at you and say "Didn't you see me bop it?" and whack it again with his nose, harder. WAIT. He may press his nose against it now and hold it there. YES - treat! Do a few then hold out for more. He'll, at some stage, press his mouth on it, then touch it with his closed teeth. YES - treat. Remember that *he's* doing the doing, not you. Don't push it at him. Position yourselves so he can easily lean forward to reach the article, which by now is so heavily loaded with rewards that it is becoming irresistible!

e. We're now working on his teeth opening, ever so slightly. Even a dog who is used to grabbing, picking up, and carrying things, will go slowly through this stage. Let him discover that what you want is for him to put his mouth round the thing. You may well get a lick as an interim stage - this is fine. So continue as you have up to now, gradually getting the article further towards being in his mouth, but always letting him decide the pace and the action. You simply reward anything that you like which is a bit further in the direction of what you want. Your dog is *taking* the article, you're not shoving it in his mouth!

As you'll have worked out by now, these steps could take many lessons. Or just a few. Always keep lessons short - maybe 3-5 minutes at most. It's important not to overface your dog. If he's slow to get it, take it slowly - at his pace, keeping the sessions short. Always finish with a bit of success (so that *you* feel you've achieved something!), and keep it all moving fast. Don't get bogged down at any stage, or he'll think that's it - that's the thing you want, a nose-touch for example. Always keep it moving along, growing.

f. At last we'll arrive at the stage where your dog opens his mouth and allows the article to go in. You need to know the place you're aiming for. It's in the gap behind the canine teeth. That's where your article can sit snugly, without irritating, without sliding about, without danger of being dropped. Don't expect a Hold at this stage! Just a split second in the mouth, even just on the tongue, is fine. And it may take a while to arrive in that correct place. This is by far the most important part of the formal retrieve, so don't rush it!

g. Your dog is now happy to see the offered article and take it in his mouth behind his canines. Remember you want the dog to be leaning forward to take the article willingly, while you hold it too. So now you can work on extending the time he holds it there. To begin with - you got it! - it's a split-second and release. You'll gradually extend the length, but always take it before his jaw muscles start to flex, he starts to dribble or in any way feel uncomfortable. As you take it you can say "Give" quietly, sometimes, then - of course - YES, treat. This is the first time you've used any vocal cue at all with him. This doesn't mean you operate in a stony silence! I chat to my dogs conversationally as I work with them.

> *I'm not doing something <u>to</u> my dog, I'm doing something <u>with</u> my dog. Big difference.*

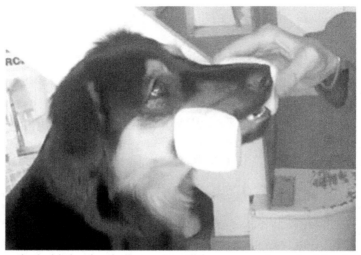

Lacy and I hold the dumbell together. What you can't see in this picture is her tail swishing! This means "Yay! I got it! I'm going to get a reward!"

3. It's absolutely ok for your dog to drop the item as soon as you say YES. You're going to get good at catching it. But to start with I would hang on to it. For one reason: you can feel instantly if there's any movement of the tongue or teeth, and say YES and remove it. For another: you're doing this together. If you're holding it there'll be no danger of it slipping or falling before you say YES. But keep in mind that you're rewarding him for releasing it. It's taken us many steps to get to this, but you're rewarding for the release. So he has to hang on till you say YES!

One way of working past an early drop is to hold the article with him to begin with, as detailed above. Then as you introduce duration you can hold it with him for 2 seconds, let go for 2 seconds, hold for 2 seconds again, then release. He'll get used to your hand advancing towards his mouth and touching the item without spitting it out.

4. Start to hold the article out a little lower for your dog to take. Then lower again. You'll need to move slightly apart for this. You could be sitting in a chair, or on the floor with her. Doesn't matter. At this stage you can let her pick it up, then YES and instantly treat. She can drop it - that's ok. Work fast and don't go for any duration. You want to teach one thing at a time, not many things at once.

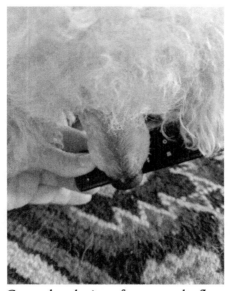

Coco takes the item from near the floor

5. Hold it very near the floor for her to take. She's got to lean down to pick it up. This is a different head movement from what she's done up to now, so give her a few reps to get the hang of it.

6. Hold it on the floor. Ensure that it's very easy for her to get her mouth round it without banging her nose. An uneven surface can help - so a mat or crumpled blanket if you're indoors. When you're out, the grass is uneven enough. To start with you mark the moment she has it, then treat for the instant release. She'll gradually learn that she can raise her head without dropping it and hand it to you.

7. Now you can toss it a very tiny distance for her to pick up. If you're working fast and rhythmically (always the best way) you can hold for pickup, repeat hold for pickup, then toss a couple of inches for pickup, and she'll do it without pause.

Coco picks up the tossed article without snatching

8. Don't start adding any distance to your throw till your dog can pick it up cleanly and hold it still in her mouth till you say YES and treat for the release. There is a real danger of building in things you don't want if you race ahead. Remember her task is to release the article to your waiting hand when you say YES, and she needs to get to that stage as quickly as she can. Focussing on the hold and release will prevent a lot of mouthing, grabbing, chomping and so on appearing in your precious retrieve!

9. If you're working towards competition, you'll need to have a wait, a release, a straight Present, and a Finish. This will all be taught on your formal competition recall then transferred to your Retrieve when what you've been doing up to now is as near perfect as can be! No confusion for your dog. If you just want your assistance dog to pick up what you've dropped, and to

fetch things for you, these parts aren't important: as long as the final hold and release are clean and considered, the rest will fall into place.

Troubleshooting

Q We're getting some chomping. I thought we were doing fine but I see the article is damaged

A Go back a few steps to where you can isolate the hold in the mouth. Maybe you went for duration and/or an active pickup a little too soon? This work is exciting for most dogs - they're keen and this can easily translate to the chomp. So fix it in the relevant step then move forward again. The system is divided up into steps so you can isolate the error and correct it in its step. Never mark your dog if he's chomping - just take the article and re-offer it. The reward comes for the clean hold/release. Try a new article too.

Q My dog has got it! So much so that he clamps on and won't let go. His mouth is tense and eyes bright

A Again, go back to a stage where you can get the instant release, before pressure or chomping can happen. It's possible his mouth is tense if you've been going too long. I aim to keep training sessions to 3-5 minutes, even with an experienced dog. The longer you go on, the more problems you can build in.

Q I can feel him squeezing the tube as I hold it when it's in his mouth. How do I fix this?

A This squeezing can be very subtle (and it will get worse), which is why I suggest holding on to the article to begin with so you can feel it straight away. Try teaching him the same sequence with a finger hold. You offer your index finger to him instead of a tube. Don't worry, your finger will survive! Go through all the same steps. If your dog has good bite inhibition he may resist taking your finger in his mouth because he has learnt that dog's teeth should never touch human skin. That's ok - you can move past this resistance and he'll hold your finger … sooo gently! You'll feel when it's in exactly the right place in his mouth.

Q As I reach for the article, he lets go before I can get it

A Holding it till you cue a release is important in competition (lots of points go for a drop!) and important when it's your phone or remote control your dog has picked up for you (smashing potential!). So this is where "proofing" the hold while you extend the duration is essential. To start with, hold-release-hold the article with him as explained above. Then you can touch the article, touch his face, his nose, wave your hands around his head, before taking it. Not all at once of course! Build up the movement gradually. You can even balance a treat on his nose or tuck one into the front of his mouth - you'll need to have good impulse control for this trick. As you get understanding you can gradually introduce these distractions. "I have to keep hanging on till I hear that word …"

Lacy keeps her hold soft even with a piece of tuna cake on her nose

Q I'm using a hard plastic tube, but it's slipping in his mouth

A Try something a bit more grippy. I was given the ridged plastic middle tube from a roll of plastic bags from the butchers - excellent article as it gives a bit of grip.

Q We started off so well, but now he doesn't seem interested

A It's important to maintain enthusiasm for this "game"! Somewhere along the line you have stopped it being fun. Perhaps you asked too much too soon, or didn't celebrate joyfully enough. I chatter as we work, with lots of "Oooh!" and "Aaah!" as we get little successes. Why should he do it at all if it's not fun for him? Work on your Play Retrieve for a while to get back the enjoyment for the task, then go back through these steps, perhaps with a different article, focussing always on your dog's level of cheery engagement.

Q We've got to him fetching the article from a distance but he's readjusting it in his mouth as he returns

A You've gone a smidgin too fast. Go back to the step where he picks it up from the ground and immediately you mark and reward. Build the duration with stillness, slowly. You may try walking backwards in front of him as he returns so he's right there, holding the item tight, waiting for you to mark and release. This shows the importance of building in the clarity of release = reward. By the way, never finish the session by tossing your article casually for him to bring back. This is where you use your play-retrieve toy, where you don't care how he holds it or tosses it. Your formal article is never played with!

In this chapter we have learnt

- The many steps that go into a formal retrieve
- The importance of rewarding the release
- You can easily correct any creeping errors in the relevant step
- "I can work this all out for myself!"

8. Adding the vocal cue

Coco is keen to retrieve when I send him

You've been working along with this so far without saying too much (I hope!). Yes to cheery chitchat, No to "commands", "orders", and the like. How would you like to be *ordered* to make a cup of tea or say hello to someone? Wouldn't you prefer to be *asked?*

Now your dog has grasped the concepts and is working confidently through the steps, we get to add some cues.

What is a cue?

A cue is something that prompts an action or chain of actions - and retrieve is nothing if not a long chain of actions. So that cue could be environmental (I open the car boot and wait for my dog to hop in, for instance), it could be a movement or gesture (you may point to the ground for a Down), or it can be a sound or word - a vocal cue.

Label the thing

Those first two cues tend to get added automatically.

The vocal cue is added deliberately, as a label for the action the dog is doing. So as your dog's bum lowers to the floor you can say "Sit" to describe it. In a short time your dog associates this new sound with the action he's making - especially if his action is rewarded in some way - and the sound "Sit" will prompt a Sit.

We need clarity in our vocal cues. It's very easy to spin them out and mess them up, confusing our poor dog! So for the retrieve I keep things simple.

What should I say?

In Tug I say "Geddit" to prompt the dog to grab the toy. In a play retrieve you don't really need a vocal cue at all, as your throwing arm movement is enough (be sure your dog is paying attention before you throw, or you'll be going to hunt for the thing yourself!). But you could use "Geddit" or your equivalent if you want.

For a competition retrieve I'd say "Hold", signifying a calmer approach to the article, a pickup with no pouncing, and carrying it without mouthing.

For around-the-house assistance-dog type retrieves, I tend to be conversational: "Pick that up for me," or "Where's my shoe?", and "Thank you," or "Thank you - where's my other shoe?" "Thank you", which also means YES, prompts the release. If the dog doesn't understand "Where's my other shoe?" wiggling the toes on my bare foot will cause the penny to drop. There really is no need to repeat cues sternly, or shout.

For the release, my hand reaching for the play retrieve toy is usually enough, though if my dog is too excited I may have to add "Give". In Tug I'll say "Give" and relax my pull which signals the dog to relax his pull and release the tug. For a competition retrieve I'd say "Give" when the steward gives the indication. In every case I want the item pushed smartly and firmly into my hand, so the same cue works for all of them.

Rollo pushes the item into my open hand. No vocal cue needed

The only other vocal cue I use is "Drop," when a muddy outside toy is about to be brought into the house! I don't want to take it, just want it left outside, so "Drop" works for this. It also works on a walk for a pine cone or ball that I can kick if it's dropped at my feet.

In all of this there's no need to sound like a drill sergeant! You can help and guide your dog to the outcome you want, as you would help and guide a young child. You don't bark commands at your three-year-old and complain when they don't get it instantly! Work *with* your dog as a team - that will bring you the quickest results.

> *Enjoy watching the learning process, the cogs whirring, the wheels turning, the connections being made and the neural pathways operating.*

Of course, you can use any words you like! As long as *you* are crystal clear in what the word means for you, and you stick to the same clear word and use it consistently. I give you my list of cues just to help you see what I mean.

Changing the cue

You may decide that for some reason you want to change the word you've been using. Perhaps a new person called "Gerrit" comes into your life and your "Geddit" won't do any more! Whatever it is, it's easy enough to change the word you're using.

Simply use the method "New cue, Old cue". This means you say the new word, let's say "Fetch" and immediately follow it with your old, known, cue, "Geddit". Continually saying "Fetch - Geddit" will soon have your dog knowing that when you say "Fetch" you actually mean "Geddit" and you can drop the old cue.

This is the same trick for teaching a dog a whistle recall - a subject that seems to fox many people. Once you have your recall trained on your vocal cue, you introduce your whistle first - "Peeep - Rover!" or "Peeep - Come," or whatever you say. Easy! There's no magic in a whistle for your recall, by the way - just that the sound carries further and cuts through wind and rain and flapping ears better.

The "poisoned cue"

Whatever is that? Well, it's when a word has acquired other meanings. If every time you called your dog you whacked him round the head when he arrived, that joyful word - his name - is going to produce very mixed feelings. You can find this quite often in rescue dogs who have had to suffer ignorance, unkindness or worse in their past.

I know a boy with learning difficulties called Jonathan. When his mother was happy with him, she'd call "Johnny!". When there was trouble looming, it would be "JonaTHAN!" Result: this uncomplicated child would only style himself 'Johnny'. He'd say "I hate 'Jonathan'". Out of the mouths of babes and little dogs …

So the simplest thing to do is start afresh with a new cue, a new name, and of course *always* a great outcome when your dog responds.

This leads to *that*. The cue predicts a possible reward. It's easy for your dog to grasp the new word when it always results in a treat, or a game.

People often tell me their dog ignores her name, however much they yell it. Take a look at this simple game, which will change all that for you:

The Precious Name Game

1. Only use your dog's name when you can pair it with good things. That means, "Fido!" - "here's a treat for you", or "Fido!" - "what a lovely doggiewoggie you are", or "Fido!" - "let's put your lead on for a walk", or "Fido!" - "here's your dinner", or "Fido!" - "grab this toy!" … you get the picture.

2. When you're frustrated or short-tempered, you find your new shoes have acquired decorative toothmarks, you need to interrupt barking in a hurry - you DON'T use his name. What do you use instead? Absolutely anything you like. From "Dog!" to "Sausages!", from "Woowoohoo!" to "&**$^**£*!!". Whatever you call, don't call his name.

If, upon sober and honest reflection, you realise that you have been colouring your dog's perception of his name - and I know how easily this can happen, especially when you're running a busy family - fear not: you can change it all.

Dogs are simple creatures. They do what works. And they learn fast.

Simply ensure that you follow 1) and 2) above. Focus on it religiously for three days and see where you are.

"Amazingly simple advice that works!"
Lisa Marie and her 8-week-old puppy

In this chapter we've learnt

- The difference between environmental and vocal cues
- Why "cue" and not "command"?
- How to add or change a vocal cue
- "I love the sound of my name!"

9. Fun

Lacy is learning to find my car keys for me - useful dog!

Hooray! We've reached the FUN chapter!

I'm going to give you some ideas of the type of fun retrieves you can teach your dog. Your dog will absolutely love being asked to do jobs for you about the house, and I'll also point out how your solid retrieve can morph into searching.

In no particular order, as the tv hosts say …

Fetch my shoes

This is so useful! Lacy will run upstairs to fetch my shoes for me when I come home. I'm always ready to reward her for her enthusiasm, speed, and joy in her work!

- Start by pointing out your shoe beside your foot - treat.
- When your dog touches the shoe - treat.
- When she puts her mouth on it - treat.
- You're going to be repeating each stage till she gets it. If your dog has been reprimanded for touching shoes in the past, you'll have to work through that first. And you may want to start with an everyday shoe, not your sparkly dancing shoes!
- Encourage her to lift her head, holding the shoe. (Shoes can be heavy)
- Let her drop it for her treat.
- Now start treating her for bringing the shoe towards you.
- Put your shoe on and watch her pleasure!
- Now you can wait while she notices something amiss - one shod foot and one naked - and races off to get the pair.

As ever, this sequence could take days, weeks, or minutes, depending on *your* speed and enthusiasm, and your ability to mark YES at the moment she *decides* to do an action (it's too late once she's done it and is thinking of the next thing).

You'll need to have a regular resting-place for your shoes so she knows where to look. Adding Hunting for the Shoes comes much later, once your dog is proficient at bringing them to you from the known place.

Where's my jumper

Another really useful one - especially if you are anchored to your chair by a cat and a whippet! Leave your jumper in an easily accessible place. Mine is usually flung over the back of the chair at my desk. If your dog is very enthusiastic I'd skip this when you want your lacy, filigree, handmade, delicate cardigan: danger of it snagging on the chair, or a tooth.

Once you've taught "Where's my shoe?" this is simply a question of identifying "jumper" and helping her find an acceptable way to carry it without treading on it.

Fetch the post

If your mail has flopped through the letterbox onto your floor this is much harder than it appears. Your dog has to pick up a flat thin envelope - possibly off a smooth hard floor, and carry it to you without ripping it or soaking it with dribble! Practice with some junk mail, so you don't care about enthusiastic accidents.

I wouldn't rip the envelope open straight away in case your dog thinks that's the next step for her. When one of my boys was just able to move about (he was a bum-shuffler, not a crawler) he fetched the mail for me, ripping it in half as he bounced along the floor with glee at his cleverness. Sadly one of the items torn in two was my puppy's International Sheepdog Society registration! So be careful what you teach …

If you have a mailbox it may be possible for your dog to open it and pull out the mail. Have fun with this!

Where's your lead?

Time for a walk? You can have your dog fetch his lead from the easily accessible place you'll park it for him. Or - a very handy trick - when you've dropped the lead or left it trailing, you can ask your dog to pick it up and press it into your hand. No need to bend!

Pick that up for me

This is my all-purpose cue for whenever I drop something - obviously only items that are safe for my dog to pick up. If I dropped a sharp knife, this would not be a time for him to scoop it up!

Many owners of assistance dogs prefer to have a default Retrieve, as they so often need help, so the dog automatically picks up anything dropped. I prefer to have a default Leave it, so that my dogs only pick things up for me when I ask. If I drop something dangerous there's no risk, though if I really had dropped a sharp knife or a headache pill I'd probably say "Leave it!" just to be sure, to be sure.

Having said that, I was so pleased to arrive home through the fields from a walk one day, to find Jake had been carrying my dropped scarf all the way back, when I hadn't even realised I'd lost it! Useful dog.

Stack the dinner bowls

If you have several dogs and dogproof bowls (mine are stainless steel) you can teach them to stack their bowls for you after they finish eating. If you've only one dog, you can just ask him to pick it up and give it to you when he's done.

Stack beakers or rings

And once they've learned to manipulate those unbreakable bowls, you can move on to more precision stuff. Toddler toys are fun here - those stacking beakers that get smaller and smaller are good for stacking inside each other. And for a real tough one, your dog can stack rings onto a pole - another favourite toddler toy. You can see Lacy putting one of the smallest rings onto the pole here (I'm holding the wobbly base still for her).

There could well be some other toys for young children which would work well - I'm not up to speed with toddlers any more! Fitting different shapes into their cut-out holes would be an advanced trick, and you'd need to have a knob on the shape big enough for the dog to grasp comfortably and manipulate easily.

Phone or tv remote

Fetching the phone or the tv remote for you require a dog who completely understands Hold as against Geddit. No chomping, mouthing, or crunching! So this is an advanced strategy. You can see Coco doing this for me here

If you want your dog to fetch your mobile phone - cellphone - for you then you need to add some kind of carrying handle or knob. Those glass screens are just too vulnerable and hard to hang on to. As soon as it starts to slip in the mouth, your dog will naturally squeeze a bit tighter … not good for expensive screens.

Modern car keys are also delicate (and expensive to replace!) so if you want your dog to fetch your keys, or retrieve them when you've dropped them, you're going to have to teach him only to hold the handle you've affixed.

Where are my keys?

Here's a complete recipe for you of how to teach this. You'll be teaching Search too - which is another great game which your dog will love, while being incredibly useful. You don't have to limit yourself to keys. You can fix your "handle" onto anything delicate you regularly need fetched. So if you skipped Chapter 7 and the Formal Retrieve, this runs you through a similar system, where it doesn't matter if your dog puts too much pressure on the handle as long as he knows not to touch the keys.

You need to start by getting some kind of soft or fluffy key fob, about tennis ball size would be good. A small soft bear would work - or you could plait some fleece to make a longer soft "handle", perhaps with a knot on the end. If your dog has a very small bite, ensure there's some small part he can hold on to. You can even scent it with a *tiny* drop of vanilla essence to enhance its powers. If your dog is very mouthy and chewy you will do well to buy or make two or three of the same keyfobs, in case one gets over-enthusiastically loved to death. You can make this key-fob much smaller once your dog has learned to pick up the keys only by the soft part of the fob.

As you now know, you'll also need some sensationally good treats - tiny cubes of cheese or hot dog usually hit the spot.

Now you can play a game with your dog with this new toy. Keep the sessions very short - maybe one or at most two minutes - and FUN!

Keys arrive unharmed!

Here's your ten-step program to a searching and retrieving wizard

1. Start by producing the key fob and holding it out to her - not in her face, just out in front of you. The second she so much as glances at it, say YES with delight (this is a game, remember!) and give her a small yummy treat. Put the toy behind your back again.

2. Repeat this peek-a-boo game until your dog is very keen to engage with this new toy and get her reward every single time it appears in view. By now you should have bright eyes and a swishing tail.

3. Hold the toy out towards her. She'll look at it and expect her treat. WAIT for just a moment, maybe waggle the toy a little, till she touches it with her nose. YES! Reward! If she bats it with her paw instead, ignore that and hold it much higher up, at nose level.

4. After a couple of nose touches, WAIT for her to put her teeth on the toy. Maybe she'll just give it a lick, or just maybe she'll open her mouth a little.

She may worry that she's not allowed to touch it, so encourage her wildly and make your YES joyful with a particularly scrummy treat. End of first session. Have a game with her with one of her own toys, and put yours safely away.

[You may need to break this down into several brief sessions. Don't push it - just get fun and a little progress each time.]

Next session, you can start again showing her the toy and rewarding her. Very quickly you can move the game forward to where you left off last time, with your dog touching the toy with some part of her mouth.

5. Using the same method, keep saying YES! and giving a tasty treat every time she touches the toy with her mouth. You can gradually encourage her to take the toy in her mouth, with you still holding on to it. End of second session.

6. You're going to advance this game, making it ever so slightly harder and ever so slightly more like a full retrieve every two or three treats. In other words, take it slowly!

7. You can start to let go of the toy, let her hold it a moment, then take it back - "Thank you!" It doesn't matter if she drops it. Graduate to holding the toy nearer to the floor for her to take; holding it on your knee, dropping it by your shoe.

Fast forward: within a few sessions you'll have a dog who gets excited at the sight of your fluffy, scented, key-fob, and who will pick it up when you drop it on the floor and smartly give it back to you to swap for her treat. Work *very quickly* and she won't even think of chomping on it.

8. Start tossing the toy further away, always rewarding her instantly for giving it back to you. Now you can add your words: "Where are my keys?" (once) every time you toss it. Always put the toy away again after each session.

9. Finally, play hunt-the-toy games. Let her watch you push it slightly under the corner of a rug (so she can actually see it to start with), then send her for

it - "Where are my keys?" Hide it under a cushion on the sofa and send her for it. Find new places to hide it, always making sure she has success and brings it straight back to you to swap for her treat. Keep this really simple - we only want success! We're not testing our dog, guys. "I know, let's put it in the biscuit tin on top of the fridge!" is not going to help one bit.

10. Attach your keys to the fluffy fob. This will make it heavier and a bit harder to balance in her mouth. Ensure she holds only the toy - if she picks up your valuable car key, just ask for it back and offer it again till she gets it. Now you can show her the toy and avert her eyes or leave her in a different room while you go and hide the toy in one of the places she's found it before. Keep it easy! She'll search all the old places till she finds it.

Keep playing this game fairly regularly - don't wait till you're in full panic having lost your keys! You know the old saying, "Use it or lose it!" When you need her to find your keys you want this exciting game to be fresh in her mind. I frequently drop things on the floor (on purpose) and ask the nearest dog to "pick that up for me". They love the opportunity to earn yet another reward!

Not only will your dog quickly learn this game of finding your keys without crunching them in her teeth, but you'll be amazed how enjoyable it is teaching her. You'll be watching the wheels go round in her head while she works out the new problem every time you move the goalposts.

> *You'll develop a new respect for your dog's abilities, and she'll love being a useful member of the family.*

Now … what other things could your dog help you with?

Picking up dropped stuff automatically

As I suggested above, I prefer my dogs to have a default Leave it, so I can decide whether the item is safe to be picked up. This is easily done! Follow the step-by-step instructions in my book *Leave It!: How to teach Amazing Impulse Control to your Brilliant Family Dog (Essential Skills for a Brilliant Family Dog Book 2)*

This will really pay off when you're walking in an area where the army holds exercises - you don't want your dog grabbing a grenade and handing it to you! (Yes, that's happened …) Similarly, and perhaps more likely, you want to get past the chip shop without your dog hoovering up the spilt chips and bringing you the empty bag.

As time goes by, your dog will know what he's asked to pick up regularly - hence Jake bringing my scarf back with him in the story earlier!

Teaching Search

This leads us on to teaching your retrieving dog to search - which you began with the keys game. One quick and easy way is to toss your play-retrieve toy into the long grass on a walk. Your dog sees where it went and will plunge in to find it. You can gradually make this a little harder (remember, softly softly - just a little tiny bit harder at a time. Don't overface your dog!) by tossing it further into the long grass, or even turning round with her to slightly disorientate her before you send her.

Gradually your dog will start to rely on her nose to find the article, rather than her eyes. Voilà! Search Dog.

If you want to teach a more formal search, you'll need to bring in a position you want the dog to adopt on finding the article while she waits for you to come and pick it up, rather than just snatching it up herself. This is so as not to destroy any evidence - or any delicate or edible item. If you're planning to compete with your dog, you'll need to do this.

But hey! - if it's just for fun - it really doesn't matter whether they grab the item or sit and stare at it. It's just another game to play with your dog, this time employing her greatest asset - her astonishing sense of smell.

Having your dog find someone's lost gloves - or worse, their car-keys! - on a country walk will impress them no end. A great chance to show off your clever dog, while saving hours of searching and panic.

In this chapter you've learnt:

- Masses of ways your dog can make life easier for you with his retrieve skills
- How to develop a greater bond with your dog
- Graduating to Search training
- "My nose is my best feature."

Conclusion

If you've worked your way through this book to here, then you must have at least the beginnings of a sensational, fast, reliable, retrieve.

If you've whizzed through the book to get a taste of it all, then you're now ready to go back and work through the steps. Choose the method most appropriate to what you want, and where you and your dog are at now.

Always remember that this is fun engagement - never a chore for your dog.

Work through … and enjoy!

Getting stuck anywhere? The **Troubleshooting** sections will help you a lot. Still stuck? Head over to the Resources section and choose one of the many ways you can get to work more with me - and get your questions answered personally!

Appreciation

I want to offer thanks to all those who have helped me get where I am with my dogs, so that I'm able to help others on the journey:

- First of all, my own long-suffering dogs! They have taught me so much when I've taken the time to listen.
- My students, who have shown me how they learn best, enabling me to give them what they need to know in a way that works for them.
- Some legendary teachers, principal amongst them: Sue Ailsby, Leslie McDevitt, Susan Garrett. I wholeheartedly recommend them. They are trailblazers.

Resources

If you've enjoyed learning about how to teach your dog to retrieve - in a reliable and kind way - and you want to find how to teach all the other skills you will need to make your dog your Brilliant Family Dog, go to www.brilliantfamilydog.com/books and choose paperback or ebook for your lap or for your reading app. The books are available worldwide through Amazon and all good bookshops (ask the bookshop to order them for you). They're all step-by-step books - I don't leave you hanging!

Calm Down! Step-by-Step to a Calm, Relaxed and Brilliant Family Dog - Book 1

Leave It! How to teach Amazing Impulse Control to your Brilliant Family Dog - Book 2

Let's Go! Enjoy Companionable Walks with your Brilliant Family Dog - Book 3

Here Boy! Step-by-Step to a Stunning Recall from your Brilliant Family Dog - Book 4

or get all four books in one volume in the Essential Skills Boxset

These cover the four skills you need to turn your wild puppy into your Brilliant Family Dog.

For a limited time, you can also get the complete first e-book in this series absolutely free! Go to www.brilliantfamilydog.com/books and you will be reading it in just a few minutes.

And if you're just starting out with your brand new puppy, and struggling to make sense of it all, here's the book for you!

New Puppy!
Biting? No sleep? Puddles?
How to survive the early weeks and still love your puppy!

I downloaded your books *Calm Down!* and *Leave It!* a few weeks ago and the change in my dog is amazing. He is learning to think about problems and his actions, learning impulse control, and he is so much calmer and happier. He's walking nicely on the lead, he's not stealing food the second I turn my back and we are working on traveling in the car and leaving the house calmly.
Anna and Toby

Very intelligent and humane training, thank you.
Jocelyn

Many thanks for your books which are wonderful - so clear and practical - I am actually looking forward to training our new pup! and establishing a harmonious joyful relationship with her.
Melissa, Australia

I love your books! Your simple, fun, and loving training methods are helping me make tremendous progress with my brilliant puppies.
Mary Anne and her two Springer pups

5* Amazon review

My dog is lovely but quite excitable, which made some things really tricky … The advice in Beverley's books is clear and simple to follow, and best of all it teaches your dog to think for itself and make good choices without any commands. We now have calm mealtimes, calm leaving the house, a brilliant recall and best of all I have given up using a headcollar, Toby now walks nicely on a loose lead and walks with him have changed from stressful, nagging ordeals into an absolute joy. Seriously, if you want a nicer, better-behaved and calmer dog, read these books and follow her steps.

The Brilliant Family dog books are amazing! I have them all. Adeline

Meanwhile, for more free training, go to www.brilliantfamilydog.com/puppies-and-dogs and get a series of instructional emails on common day-to-day problems like jumping up, chewing, barking, and so on.

Your emails are absolutely wonderful! I love them. Nobody else does anything like this. Maggie and Archie

The one thing Busta wasn't so good at was greeting people, but since your email we've had everyone popping in to put your tips into place and it worked! Now we no longer have him jumping all over us when we come through the door. Just a very happy dog sat down waggling his tail like mad, waiting for a fuss! Charlie and Busta

Thank you for sharing your wisdom with us new puppy owners! Although I grew up with dogs and our puppy is our second family dog it doesn't make it any easier!
Sarah

First let me tell you that your housetraining advice was AMAZING. I practiced everything you suggested and within 1-2 days, I had no more accidents in the house. I am thrilled with the practical suggestions, methods and techniques that you have made available on the internet. Your wealth of experience is amazing and your willingness to share it is wonderful. Thank you for what you do.
Elizabeth and Ruby

Hey Beverley, loving being part of your gang!
Sonia and Benson

I am loving your emails and you are covering many issues that I have with my 9 month old Cockerpoo.
Kerry and Meg

COURSES

For more in-depth training - and a wonderful way you can get personalised coaching from anywhere in the world! - check out these two courses at brilliantfamilydog.teachable.com

From Wild Puppy to Brilliant Family Dog (for puppies up to about 9 months)

From Challenging Dog to Brilliant Family Dog (for dogs over 9 months or so)

With over 50 daily videos, an amazingly enthusiastic and supportive private training group, and permanent access, you can join other students from all round the world in changing your relationship with your puppy!

> Hello there! Snoopy (our Kelpie puppy) completed this brilliant course with flying colours. The course was amazing and I have highly recommended it to others! We continue to do many of the exercises as just so positive, practical and effective!
> Rebecca and Snoopy, student on From Wild Puppy to Brilliant Family Dog

> Can't believe how far Echo has come from being terrified of other people, dogs and new sights and experiences. So proud of her. She is listening to me more when we are closer to another person or dog and her recall has been remarked upon by other dog walkers! Our

relationship has grown by leaps and bounds doing this course. She has brought so much love and magic to my life and even more so having found your course and books as it has decreased my stress so I'm able to enjoy her more. From wild puppy to engaging companion!

Cluny and Echo, student on From Wild Puppy to Brilliant Family Dog

You will LOVE this course, and one of the many great things about it is you can do it at your own and your dog's pace. No pressure! I am so grateful to Beverley for the knowledge she has given me on how to communicate with my dogs.

Patricia, student on From Challenging Dog to Brilliant Family Dog

Impressive set of dogs you've got and you have been teaching us much! No way I would've have survived without your knowledge - thanks again.

Amal, student on From Challenging Dog to Brilliant Family Dog

If you have a dog who is reactive, anxious or fearful of everything, especially other dogs, you can find lots of resources to help you at
www.brilliantfamilydog.com/growly-dogs

and there's a course just for you - at brilliantfamilydog.teachable.com

And if you've got any specific queries, you can email me direct at beverley@brilliantfamilydog.com This will come straight to my personal inbox and I'll answer you - usually within 48 hours.
Try me!

RESOURCES

Chapter 2

For UK readers - 75% off your first big box of homecooked food at www.butternutbox.com/brilliantfamilydog *

For UK readers - 50% off quality tinned and dry dog food at www.bobandlush.com/beverleyc *

* If you purchase through these links I will benefit - but you'll benefit more!

Chapter 6

Lacy plays Retrieve Games

http://www.brilliantfamilydog.com/retrieve

Don't go without your free book!

Get the next piece of the puzzle for your dog

Get the first digital book in the series,
Essential Skills for your Brilliant Family Dog
absolutely free here
https://www.brilliantfamilydog.com/freebook-calm-down

About the Author

I've been training dogs for many years. First for competitive dog sports and over time to be stellar family pets. For most of my life, I've lived with up to four dogs at a time, so I'm well used to getting a multi-dog household to run smoothly. It soon became clear that a force-free approach was by far the most successful, effective, and rewarding for me and the dogs.

I've done the necessary studying for my various qualifications - for rehab of anxious and fearful "aggressive" dogs, early puppy development, and learning theory and its practical applications. I am continually studying and learning this endlessly amazing subject!

There are some superb teachers and advocates of force-free dog training, and you'll find those I am particularly indebted to in the Resources Section. Some of the methods I show you are well-known in the force-free dog training community, while many have my own particular twist.

A lot of my learning has come through the Puppy Classes, Tutored Puppy Walks, and Starter Classes I teach. These dog-owners are not looking for competition-standard training; they just want a Brilliant Family Dog they can take anywhere. More recently I've been able to extend my understanding by interacting with readers of my books, and with students of my busy online courses, and delight in the change they are able to achieve.

Working with real dogs and their real owners keeps me humble - and resourceful! It's no good being brilliant at training dogs if you can't convey this enthusiasm and knowledge to the person the dog has to live with. So I'm grateful for everything my students have taught me about how they learn best.

Beverley Courtney
BA(Hons), CBATI, CAP2, MAPDT(UK), ABTC Registered Animal Instructor

Printed in Great Britain
by Amazon

86558648R00062